Introduction

The activity pages in this book are designed to be used with 5 to 6 year olds. In particular, they are intended to support the programmes on **Numbers and the Number System** in the Channel 4 Schools maths series **The Number Crew**.

The general aim of the book is to provide a stimulating mix of activities to develop numeracy work in the classroom and at home. It can be used to help children develop mental methods, learn the language of numbers, and move beyond counting to explore and use relationships to learn number facts.

For those teachers engaged in Numeracy Lessons, each programme provides a whole-class focus on a particular mathematical idea. The activity sheets can then be used as extensions. They can be photocopied, given out and then talked through with the children working in groups or individually.

There are ten sections in the book, each of which supports and extends the content of the programmes.

1 All Aboard

Reciting in order the numbers from 0 to 20 and back again.

2 Numbers on the Doors

Reading and writing the numbers up to 20.

3 The Welcome Meeting

Counting at least 20 objects (last number gives the count), and understanding that if the objects are rearranged the number stays the same.

4 Storm and Seasickness 1

Counting on and back in ones from any number under ten.

5 Storm and Seasickness 2

Counting on and back in tens to and from 100.

6 Time for Treats

Knowing what a two-digit number represents.

7 The Dancing Bear

Saying the number that is 1 or 10 more than a given number.

8 Drinks for All

Counting on and back in twos and beginning to recognise odd and even numbers.

9 Hunting for Bunting

Counting on and back in fives.

10 The Party

Comparing and ordering, includir

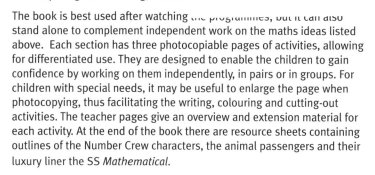

The book is best used after watching the programmes, but it can also stand alone to complement independent work on the maths ideas listed above. Each section has three photocopiable pages of activities, allowing for differentiated use. They are designed to enable the children to gain confidence by working on them independently, in pairs or in groups. For children with special needs, it may be useful to enlarge the page when photocopying, thus facilitating the writing, colouring and cutting-out activities. The teacher pages give an overview and extension material for each activity. At the end of the book there are resource sheets containing outlines of the Number Crew characters, the animal passengers and their luxury liner the SS *Mathematical*.

You may find it useful to:

- Look at the activity sheets first – although they follow the programmes in consecutive order, the suggested activities can easily be slotted in any order into your own teaching scheme.

- Adapt the sheets to suit the needs of your class – blank out, amend or add parts as you think fit.

- Talk the children through the sheets first before using them.

- Encourage the children to read the sheets to themselves and to one another as they use them.

- Let the children use the backs of the sheets for extension work related to the completed activity on the front.

- Have fun and enjoy maths.

Contents

GW00599270

Teacher's Notes

All Aboard

1.1 Count Up

Aim: to develop accurate oral counting from 1 to 20 and back.

Encourage children to say the words as they point to the numbers on the sheet.

Extensions: Use appropriate traditional rhymes like 'One, two, buckle my shoe', and adapt other rhymes to use larger numbers – for example, '20 green bottles'.

1.2 How Many Animals?

Aims: to teach children to count on from a given small number; to develop problem-solving skills.

Ask who can count on 3 starting at 5? At 10? At 15? Talk about quick ways to answer the problem.

Extension: Extend counting skills – for example, starting at 24 count on 3; starting at 26 count back 5.

1.3 How Many Meals?

Aim: to develop problem-solving skills.

Encourage the children to name all 20 animal passengers. Check that they know the family members of the Number Crew (see page 40). Ask how to work out the number of meals needed altogether. Remind the children that it is sensible to start from the biggest number when counting on.

Extensions: Ask how many meals would be needed if there were 7, 8, or 10 in the family. Let the children explore ways to check their answers.

Numbers on the Doors

2.1 Joining Up

Aim: to improve number recognition.

Before giving out the sheet, encourage the class to count in unison up to 50. Suggest that they say the numbers to themselves as they join the dots. What is the picture?

Extensions: Children could make their own dot-to-dot pictures. Or they could write numbers on unmarked number lines.

2.2 Words and Numbers

Aim: recognition of number names.

Talk about the number names which should already be familiar. Encourage the children to look for patterns such as 'teen' as they do the activity.

Extensions: Make cards with number words up to 30 or 40. Share them among the class and ask the children to say their number and find it on a number line. Children could work in pairs with a selection of number name cards and match them to the correct number of counting cubes.

2.3 Snake Numbers

Aim: to read and write numbers.

Talk about how two-digit numbers are written. Make sure the children start all numbers from the top. Remind the children that when writing 'teen' numbers the '1' stands for one ten and comes first.

Extensions: Children could draw a longer snake, using strips of squared paper. Ask them to write numbers in order as far as they can. This is a good assessment activity. Some children could match number names and symbols.

© 1998 Channel Four Learning

Count Up

The Number Crew have loads of passengers. How many do they have?

They've got

1, 2, 3 passengers

4, 5, 6 passengers

7, 8, 9 passengers

and one more makes 10

11, 12, 13 passengers

14, 15, 16 passengers

17, 18, 19 passengers

20 all in all

Point to the numbers as you say the rhyme.

All Aboard (1.1)

© 1998 Channel Four Learning

How Many Animals?

How many animal passengers are on the ship?

How many animals are on the gangway?

How many animals are there altogether?

© 1998 Channel Four Learning

All Aboard (1.2)

How Many Meals?

It is lunchtime on board.

How many meals are needed? ☐

© 1998 Channel Four Learning

Joining Up

Join the numbers.

© 1998 Channel Four Learning

Numbers on the Doors (2.1)

Words and Numbers

Join the numbers.

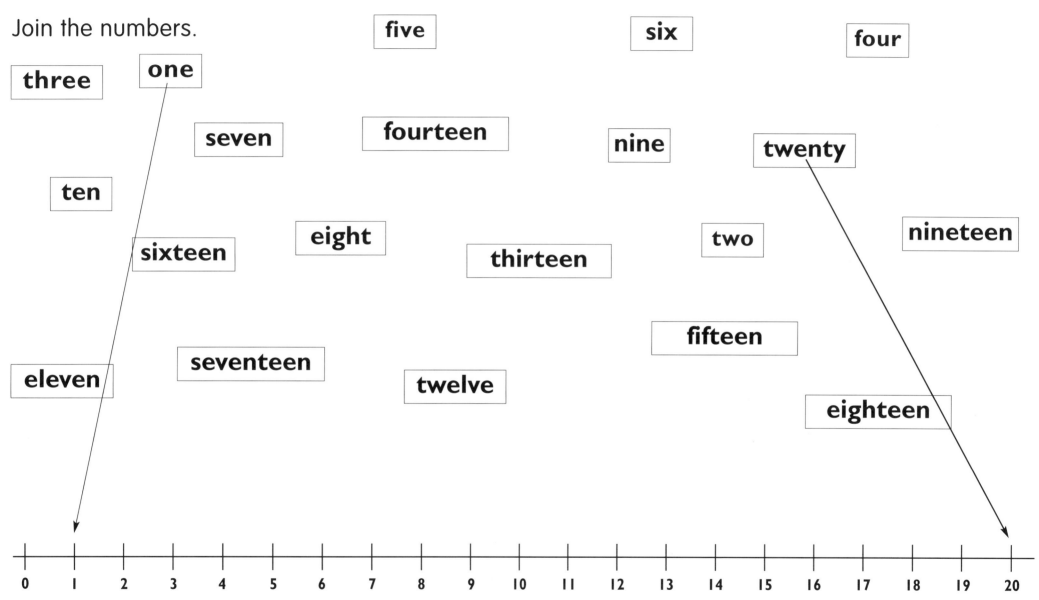

Join the words and numbers.

Snake Numbers

Write the missing numbers.

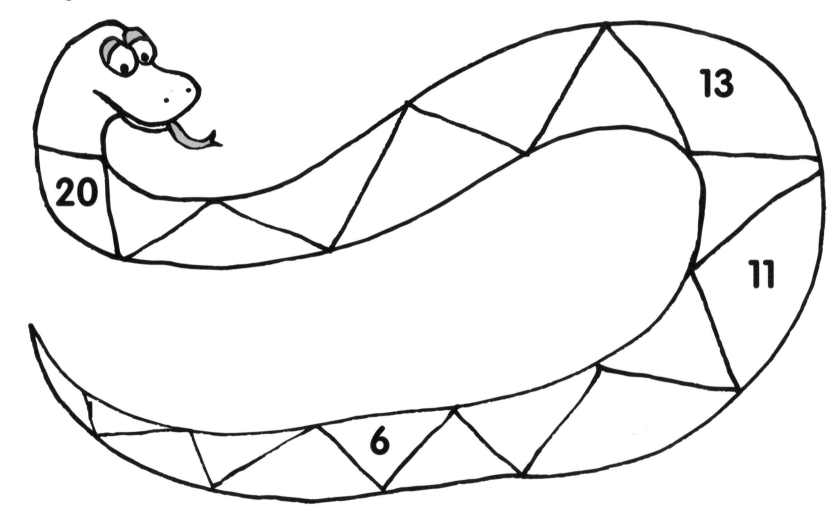

© 1998 Channel Four Learning

Numbers on the Doors (2.3)

Teacher's Notes

The Welcome Meeting

3.1 Hands and Feet

Aim: to encourage the use of digits when counting.

Talk about the word 'digit' and the link with fingers and toes. Count in fives and tens, opening the fingers as the numbers are said. Relate to rhymes such as 'Ten little fingers, ten little toes'.

Extensions: Give the children collections of buttons, shells or beads to count by grouping in fives or tens. Some children could be introduced to 'tallying'.

3.2 More and More

Aim: to encourage efficient counting.

Talk about the problem with the children and let them suggest ways of solving it. How can they check their answers?

Extensions: Have a collection of pennies for the children to count in piles of 5. Have some 5p coins as well. Demonstrate how the coins can be counted quickly to find out how much money there is. Some children could work in pairs to count piles of 10p.

3.3 Hidden Numbers

Aim: to raise awareness of the numbers in the fives sequence.

Count in fives with the class. Talk about the grid and ask where the fives numbers are found. Ask if the children know why.

Extensions: Ask the children to explain their strategies for deciding which numbers are covered. Repeat the exercise, using grids with some numbers missing.

Storm and Seasickness 1

4.1 Missing Numbers

Aim: to encourage counting on.

Let the class count in ones starting from different numbers. Work with a class number line. Ask individual children if they can carry on the sequence. Talk about numbers 'after', 'before' and 'between'.

Extension: Children can work in pairs with a 'washing' number line and take turns to ask for number cards, giving clues like 'the number after 6', 'the number before 20' and so on.

4.2 Number Shells

Aim: to revise simple known number sequences.

Count forwards and backwards in ones starting at different numbers. Use a class number line. Ask individual children to suggest sequences and others to demonstrate them.

Extensions: Children work in pairs to give each other sequences of numbers to continue. More able children can use larger numbers. Calculators, if set to use the 'constant' function, can be used as a check.

4.3 Forwards and Backwards

Aim: to encourage accuracy of counting.

Have whole-class sessions of oral counting with and without a number line. Say a number and ask the children to count on 1, then 2, and so on. When they are confident with counting on, start counting back.

Extension: Children work in pairs to play a game using a number grid with missing numbers. One child points at a point on the grid and the other says the missing number. If it is correct, he or she covers the number with a coloured cube. The person with the most cubes on the grid at the end of the game is the winner.

© 1998 Channel Four Learning

Hands and Feet

Draw round your hands. Count the fingers. Count the thumbs.

How many digits on your hands? ☐

How many digits on your feet? ☐

How many digits altogether? ☐

© 1998 Channel Four Learning

More and More

1. Here are some animals.
   Count them. ☐

2. Some more arrive.
   How many animals are there now? ☐

3. The last group of animals arrive.
   How many are there altogether? ☐

© 1998 Channel Four Learning

Hidden Numbers

Work in pairs and take turns.

1 Cover some numbers with counters.

2 Ask your partner which numbers are covered.

3 Check by removing the counters.

1	2	3	4	5
6	7	8	9	10
11	12	13	14	15
16	17	18	19	20
21	22	23	24	25

© 1998 Channel Four Learning   The Welcome Meeting (3.3)

Missing Numbers

Fill in the missing numbers.

What are the next ten numbers?

Number Shells

Write the next three numbers in each shell.

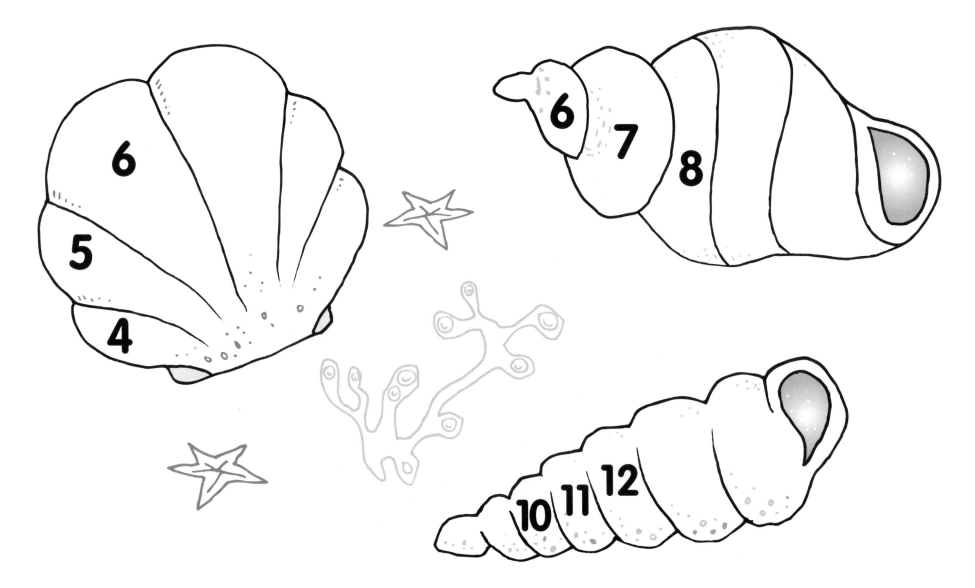

© 1998 Channel Four Learning

Forwards and Backwards

 Start at 4, count on 3.   **7**   

 Start at 2, count on 5.

 Start at 6, count on 6.

 Start at 12, count back 7.

 Start at 15, count back 5.

 Start at 20, count back 9.

Teacher's Notes

Storm and Seasickness 2

5.1 Digit Sums

Aim: to count on and back in tens.

Talk about fingers and toes and the word 'digit'. Ask the children how many digits they have altogether. Count in tens to 100. Then count back in tens. Read through the activity sheet with the children.

Extensions: Children could be asked to find the number of digits in the whole class. Working in pairs, children could give each other 'digit' problems, like 'how many digits does your family have?'

5.2 Ten Down

Aim: to count back in tens from different starting numbers.

A large number line or 100 square would be a good focus for talking about counting back in tens. For example, start at 57 and count back 10 to 47, then 37 and so on. Point out which of the digits changes.

Extensions: Some children could start from numbers beyond 100. Working in pairs, children could ask partners to count back in tens from any number. A calculator using the 'constant' function could be used as a check.

5.3 Across and Down

Aim: to recognise the effect on numbers of counting on or back in tens.

Talk about the numbers found on a 100 square and make sure the children realise that if the grid is 10 wide then the numbers in each column increase by 10. They should be able to work out the missing numbers by adding 10 to the numbers given.

Extension: Some children could use numbers beyond 100. Play the game 'what number am I thinking of?' giving clues such as 'my number is 10 more than 11' or 'my number is 10 less than 92'.

Time for Treats

6.1 Pocket Money

Aim: to teach children what a two-digit number represents.

Talk about the advantages of using 10p coins. Children should understand that one 10p coin can be exchanged for ten 1p coins. Revise counting in tens. Check that children recognise twenty as 'two tens' and thirty as 'three tens', and can separate numbers like 34 into 30 and 4. Have coins available if needed.

Extension: Children could be given larger sums of money to count, including 20p coins.

6.2 Finish the Sums

Aim: to teach children what a two-digit number represents.

Remind the children of the song about two-digit numbers in the programme. (The words and music are in the Teachers' Guide.) Use place-value cards with the whole class and ask the children to show you' numbers such as 34, 56 and 27 by placing the tens and units cards together.

Extension: The children need a selection of cards with numbers up to 100, placed face down, and a set of place-value cards. Working in pairs, they take turns to pick up a number card and say the number. The other child makes the number with place-value cards and writes it down.

6.3 Number Skittles

Aim: to consolidate work on two-digit numbers.

Talk about the activity. Check that the children understand how to operate their calculator to key in and 'knock down' the skittle numbers.

Extension: The same game can be played with three-digit numbers.

© 1998 Channel Four Learning

Digit Sums

Here is the Number Crew.

Everyone has 10 hand digits (fingers) and 10 foot digits (toes).

How many digits does Baby Bunting have?

How many digits do Ted and Mirabelle have together?

How many digits do Fiz, Flo and Bradley have altogether?

What about the whole family?

Ten Down

Count back in tens down each snake.

© 1998 Channel Four Learning

Storm and Seasickness 2 (5.2)

Across and Down

	1	2	3	4	5	6	7	8	9
10				14					
				24					
				34					
				44					

Fill in the missing numbers.

Pocket Money

How much money does each person have?

Here are the coins they have:	10p coins	1p coins		
TEN PENCE 10, TEN PENCE 10, TEN PENCE 10, ONE PENNY 1, ONE PENNY 1	3	2	Bradley has	32 p
TEN PENCE 10, TEN PENCE 10, ONE PENNY 1, ONE PENNY 1, ONE PENNY 1			Fiz has	p
TEN PENCE 10, TEN PENCE 10, TEN PENCE 10, TEN PENCE 10, ONE PENNY 1			Flo has	p
TEN PENCE 10, TEN PENCE 10, TEN PENCE 10, TEN PENCE 10, TEN PENCE 10			Baby has	p

Time for Treats (6.1)   © 1998 Channel Four Learning

Finish the Sums

Write the missing numbers.

$25 = 20$ and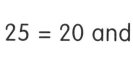

$13 = 10$ and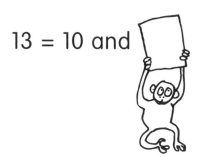

$35 =$  and 5

$42 = 40$ and

$14 = 10$ and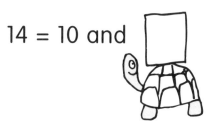

$51 =$ 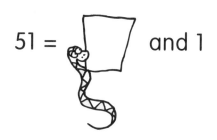 and 1

$17 = 10$ and

$17 =$ 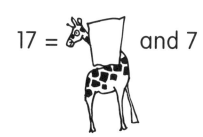 and 7

$64 = 60$ and

© 1998 Channel Four Learning

Time for Treats (6.2)

Number Skittles

Work in pairs and take turns. Use a calculator and coloured pencils.

One person chooses a skittle number and keys it into the calculator.

The other person tries to 'knock down' the number to 0 one digit at a time using the ⊟ key.

Colour the skittle in your chosen colour when you reach 0.

The winner is the person with the most coloured skittles.

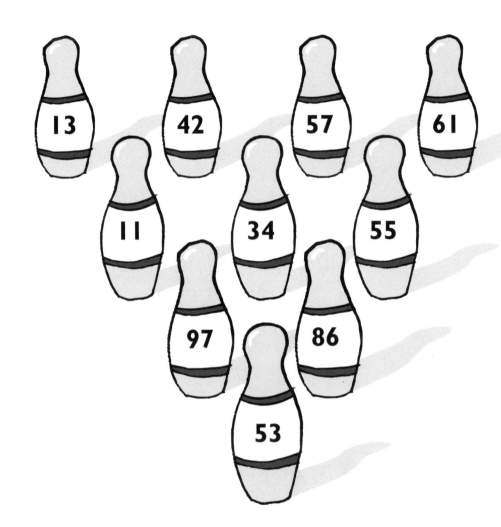

© 1998 Channel Four Learning

Teacher's Notes

The Dancing Bear

7.1 Boats

Aim: to help children recognise numbers one more than a given number.

Spend a few minutes counting orally in ones, starting at any number. Use a 100 square as a focus for the counting.

Extension: A similar activity could be prepared with starting numbers only.

7.2 More Boats

Aim: to recognise numbers ten more than a given number.

Spend a few minutes counting orally in tens, starting at any number. Use a 100 square as a focus for the counting.

Extension: A similar activity could be prepared with starting numbers only.

7.3 On and On

Aim: to write numbers 1 or 10 more than a given number.

Ask the children for the number 'one more than' a selection of starting numbers beginning at one, and the number 'ten more than' a selection of starting numbers beginning at 10. Talk about the different numbers obtained.

Extension: A group or whole-class game. Have a selection of number cards in a bag. Children sit in a circle and pass the bag round. Each in turn takes out a card and says the number. You then ask for the number 'one more than', or 'ten more than' that number. If correct, the child keeps the card. Continue until all the cards have been taken.

Drinks for All

8.1 Even Stevens

Aim: to recognise even numbers under 100.

Ask the children if they can give you an even number less than 100. If some children are uncertain, spend some time counting orally in ones to 100. Whisper the odd numbers and clap on the even numbers. Some children may need more practical experience with cubes or buttons.

Extension: Numbers can be extended beyond 100. Explore the unit digits pattern in even numbers.

8.2 Very Odd

Aim: to recognise a sequence of odd numbers under 100.

Ask the children for examples of odd numbers less than 100. Spend some time counting odd numbers to 100. Emphasise the sequence 1, 3, 5, 7, 9.

Extension: Numbers can be extended beyond 100. Explore the unit digits pattern in odd numbers.

8.3 Odd and Even

Aim: to recognise odd and even numbers.

Talk about the pattern of alternate odd and even numbers. Ask what numbers come next in the sequences 11, 13, 15... or 20, 18, 16.... Do some oral counting before giving out the activity sheet.

Extension: Numbers can be extended beyond 100.

© 1998 Channel Four Learning

Boats

Match pairs of boats.

© 1998 Channel Four Learning

The Dancing Bear (7.1)

More Boats

Match pairs of boats.

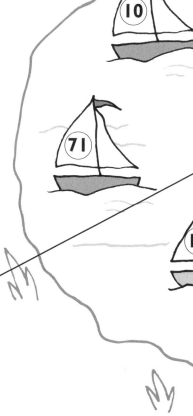

is 10 more than

On and On

Complete the boxes.
Check with a calculator.

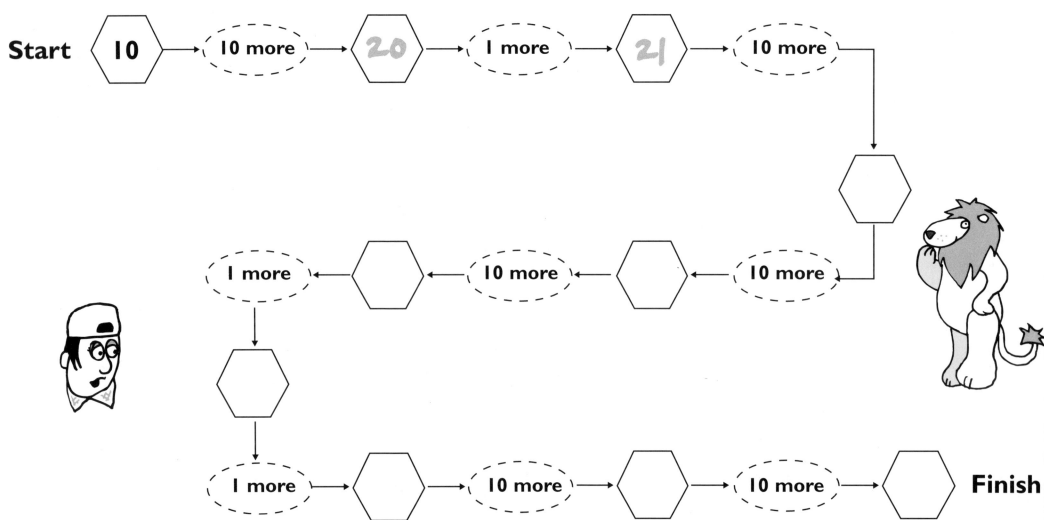

Start ⟨ 10 ⟩ → (10 more) → ⟨ 20 ⟩ → (1 more) → ⟨ 21 ⟩ → (10 more) →

⟨ ⟩

(1 more) ← ⟨ ⟩ ← (10 more) ← ⟨ ⟩ ← (10 more) ←

⟨ ⟩

(1 more) → ⟨ ⟩ → (10 more) → ⟨ ⟩ → (10 more) → ⟨ ⟩ **Finish**

© 1998 Channel Four Learning

The Dancing Bear (7.3)

Even Stevens

Join the **even** numbers.

Remember even numbers end with 0, 2, 4, 6 or 8.

Drinks for All (8.1)

© 1998 Channel Four Learning

Very Odd

Complete this **odd**-numbered track.

© 1998 Channel Four Learning

Drinks for All (8.2)

Odd and Even

Colour the **even**-numbered parts.

Then use a **different** colour for the **odd**-numbered parts.

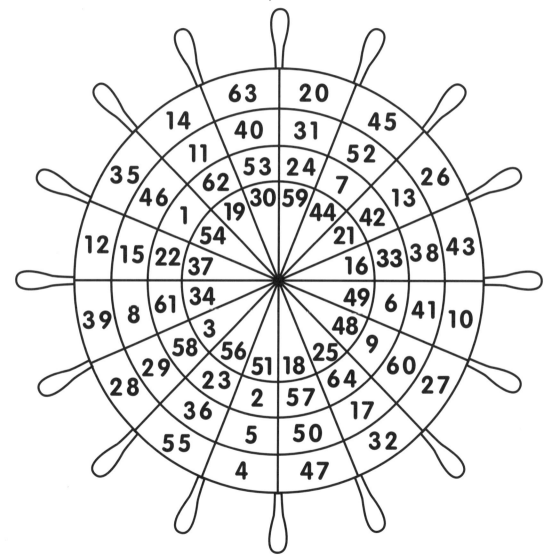

Teacher's Notes

Hunting for Bunting

9.1 Number Crunching

Aim: to help children recognise the fives numbers.

Spend a few minutes with the whole class counting orally in fives to 100. Use a class number line or 100 square to focus the counting.

Extension: Use the completed activity sheet as the basis of a game for two players. Cover the numbers on the left of the machine with counters. Children take turns to choose a number on the right and say the link number on the left. Check by removing the counter. If correct the counter is kept. The one with most counters when all the numbers are uncovered is the winner.

9.2 More Number Crunching

Aim: to help children count back in fives.

As a whole class, count backwards in fives, starting from 20, then from 50. Then ask the children for numbers 'five less than' a given number in the fives sequence. Make sure the children understand the instructions on the sheet.

Extension: Make a game from the completed sheet, as in 9.1 above.

9.3 In Fives

Aim: to help children count on and back in fives.

Demonstrate on a class number line the hops that Baby Bunting would make. Ask the children to say the numbers as you point to them.

Extension: Extend the number lines to include larger numbers. Ask children to colour in the fives numbers.

The Party

10.1 Queuing Up

Aim: to help children use ordinal numbers.

Talk about the sequence of events during the children's day. Encourage children to use the vocabulary of ordering events, such as 'first', 'second' and 'last'. Talk through the events of Baby Bunting's day before giving the children the sheet.

Extension: The children could be asked to draw pictures of events in their day at school.

10.2 Baby Bunting's Day

Aim: to help children use ordinal numbers.

Talk about queuing. Select a few children to form a queue at the front of the class to demonstrate the 'position' words.

Extension: Use informal opportunities, for example when children are lining up for assembly or lunch, for them to state their position. Some children may need help with bigger numbers such as 'thirty-first' or 'thirty-second'.

10.3 Rosettes

Aim: to help children use ordinal numbers.

Talk about a sports day, or other events such as a swimming gala or horse show, where rosettes are awarded to people or animals who win races.

Extension: Ask the children to match the ordinal words to the symbols.

© 1998 Channel Four Learning

Number Crunching

Write, in order, the numbers as they come out of the machine.
The first one has been done for you.

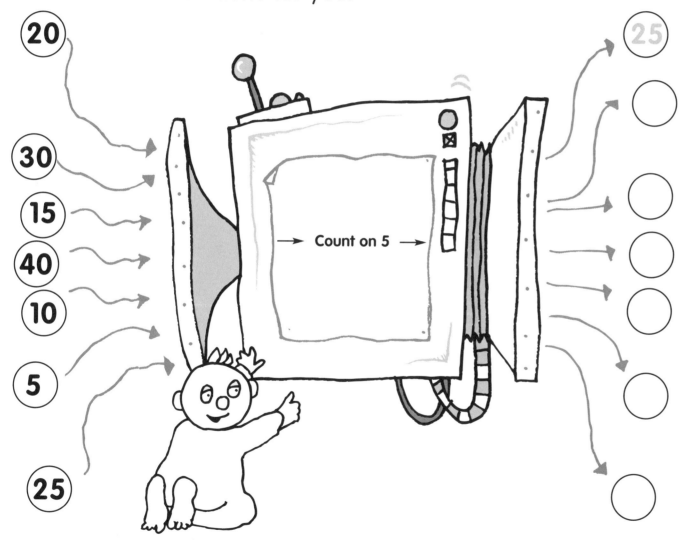

© 1998 Channel Four Learning

More Number Crunching

Write, in order, the numbers as they come out of the machine.

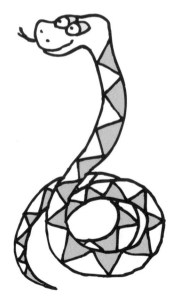

© 1998 Channel Four Learning

Name   Date

In Fives

Baby Bunting jumps forward in fives. Circle the numbers he lands on.

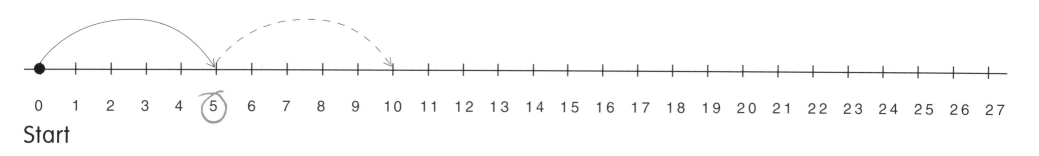

Start

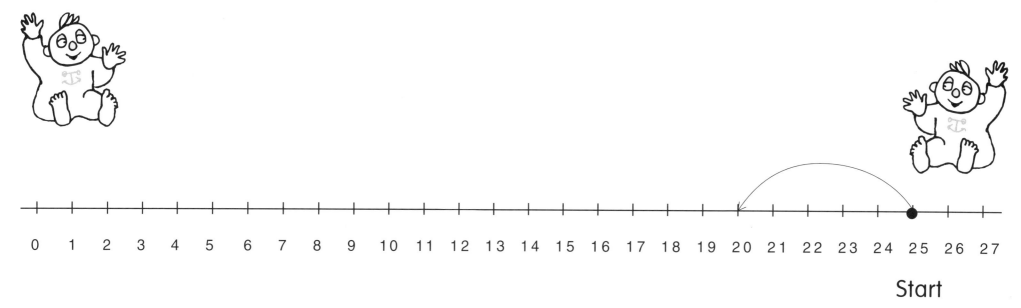

Start

He now jumps back in fives.

Circle the numbers he lands on.

Queuing Up

The animals queue for their prizes.

Crocodile is the **first** in the queue.

_____ is the **second** in the queue.

_____ is the **fourth** in the queue.

Who is the **third**? _____

© 1998 Channel Four Learning   The Party (10.1)

Baby Bunting's Day

Cut along the dotted lines. Put the pictures in order. Match them with the words.

Rosettes

Cut out the rosettes.

Colour them.

Give them to the animals in the right order.

© 1998 Channel Four Learning   The Party (10.3)

Resource Sheet

The SS *Mathematical*

© 1998 Channel Four Learning

Resource Sheet

The Animals (1)

lion

moose

monkey

panda

gorilla

camel

hippo

penguin

giraffe

tiger

© 1998 Channel Four Learning

Resource Sheet

The Animals (2)

snake
rhino
polar bear
elephant
zebra
kangaroo
buffalo
ostrich
crocodile
turtle

© 1998 Channel Four Learning

Resource Sheet

The Number Crew

Ted

Mirabelle

Flo

Fiz

Bradley

Baby Bunting

© 1998 Channel Four Learning